THE DISCIPLES SHARE THE WORD

THE DISCIPLES SHARE THE WORD

Witnessing to the Word of God

Ishmael "Mac"McDonald

authorHOUSE®

DEDICATION

This book is written in memory of, and dedicated, to, my mother Susan McDonald (nee) McDonald, and my father William Hawley McDonald, both of whom loved, nurtured, and advised me all of their lives, yes, and disciplined me in my youth.

Also in memory of, The Reverend Frank Wilkerson, who encouraged me to preach my first sermon, and to honor Reverend Bert Pitchford, who, has been my dear friend, pastor, and advisor for these last thirty years.

I owe them all a debt of gratitude, that I can never repay, and I thank God for what they all have done for me.

ENDORSEMENT

Ishmael "Mac" McDonald's book

When Mac called me, and told me he had written a book, I must say I was a bit surprised. Few persons have the courage to attempt such a task. I was curious as to what I would find as I read a copy of the manuscript he handed me. It was not that thick, so I didn't think it would overwhelm me to read it. I must warn you, it is not a profound masterpiece of theology. It is simple, yet profoundly filled with a man's sincere desire to preach the Word of God, as Mac feels the Holy Spirit has called him to do.

This little book does not contain anything new, or earthshaking, but then, that was not Mac's purpose. His purpose is simply to reveal God's love, through His Word (both written and living).

The underlying theme, in this book, is to emphasize the power of the Holy Spirit to work within, and through, "The Word.".

This book is about Mac's sincere love for his God, who not only created him, but has blessed him with the gift of eternal life, through his only begotten Son, Christ our Savior, through the Scriptures from the creation of the world, Genesis 1;1,to creation of "new life" in each of us 2d Corinthians 5:17. It is apparent that Mac's desire is that everyone who reads what he has written will be as convicted by God's Holy Spirit, as he has been; and that the reader will be moved to share God's Word; till he comes again *signed*: Bert Pitchford

Mac's old Pastor, and friend.

QUOTATION

"What the Church needs now are active Disciples, who are obsessed by the Holy Spirit to go out, and make others to become *Disciples*, along the way."

Mac

INTRODUCTION

I, Ishmael McDonald, was born on November the third in Harnett County, North Carolina, the son of a farmer. I was married to my wife, Clara, and we had a beautiful daughter, Linda Ann, soon after my twenty-fourth birthday. I spent a good deal of my time and energy struggling to provide a comfortable living for my family before I preached my first sermon, which led me to become a certified lay pastor in the Presbyterian church.

I made a profession of faith and became a member of Flat Branch Presbyterian Church in 1936 and was elected an elder in 1955. I was a very introverted person. But when I became a member of the session I thought there must be something I could do for the Lord, besides voting on the issues that came before the session. I earnestly began praying the Lord would lead me so I might lead others.

I taught Sunday school until the pastor, Rev. Frank Wilkerson, asked me to lead a service in his absence. I declined, saying I would do anything for him, but I could not do that. On his insistence I preached my first sermon and began filling other pulpits when requested; I was soon placed on the Coastal Carolina Presbyteries' list of approved elders to preach in other churches. When the presbytery conducted a school for certified lay preachers, I was one of the first laymen to be certified to pastor a church. I was certified as pastor of the First Presbyterian Church in Erwin, North Carolina.

In February 2002 I was called by the Palestine Presbyterian Church in Linden, North Carolina, where I am serving at the time of this writing. And where I was I was led, by the Holy Spirit to preach the sermons, on which this book is based.

I was elected Elder Emeritus of the Flat Branch Church in 2011, where I grew up, and am still a member.

On January 6th, 2013 I was honored when the membership of the church elected me Pastor Emeritus, of Palestine Presbyterian church, at 8081 Ramsey, Street, Linden, NC. After eleven years of being honored to serve these people, I have' learned to love them, as bothers, and sisters in Christ, and I expect to still serve the church as a supply Pastor, when needed

I suspect that someone might wonder how a full-blooded, Scot preacher with a surname of, McDonald came to have an Islamic name, Ishmael. I was the firstborn of William Hawley McDonald and my dear mother, Susan McDonald. My father wished to name me after his father, Hugh Dallas, but my mother, who was a lot younger than my father, had read a book in which Ishmael was her Hero, and was determined to name me Ishmael. She told Daddy he could add any name he chose. My daddy said, "I think that's enough," so I was not given a middle name. Twelve years later my younger brother ended up with the name my father wished to give me.

My name bothered me tremendously. When I was in school all of my classmates teased me and called me all kinds of names. It was so unbearable that I wished to change my name officially when I came of age.

But before that day arrived I learned about a man in Smithfield, North Carolina, whose family name was Hood, and his father had named him Robin. He had grown up facing the same problems I faced all through public school and was equally ashamed of his name. When he entered Campbell College, on the first day a professor suggested they should each introduce themselves to the class. When it came to Robin's turn he was so embarrassed he could hardly speak, but he stammered out "Robin Hood. When the class was over the professor asked Robin to stay and talk to him. He told him he had noticed his embarrassment and gave him some advice, saying, "You can go through life timid and ashamed of your name Robin Hood, or you can capitalize on it."

When as a teenager I heard this true story, the town of, Smithfield, N C was overrun with businesses bearing the name Robin Hood. This caused me to forget about changing my name. Besides I knew it would have broken my Dear Mother's heart, and now most of my friends call me Mac.

When I was in a school for Lay Pastors an Old Testament professor assigned a lesson for each of us. We were to assume the character of an Old Testament person and write an essay using the first person singular as our topic. I naturally chose Ishmael, and here is a copy of my article.

My name is Ishmael. I have been called by some a wild man. My father, Abraham, made a covenant with God, and God promised him that his descendants would be numerous. He promised God that he would walk in

His ways, and God promised that he and his descendants would be blessed.

My father and his wife, Sarah, had become old. Sarah was well past normal child-bearing age. When Sarah had no children she gave my mother, Hagar, her handmaiden, to my father that, she might conceive and bear him a son. When it became evident that my mother was with child she began to love my father and despise Sarah. Sarah made it difficult for my mother, who then fled to her homeland in Egypt. But an Angel of the Lord intercepted her and instructed her to return and submit to Sarah, her mistress. He encouraged her and promised that her descendants through me, her son Ishmael, would be many. I was circumcised at the age of thirteen according to the covenant my father had made with God.

At that time my father exclaimed to God, that Ishmael might live before Him, and serve Him. Sarah conceived and bore my father a son who was named Isaac, which means one who laughs, because my father and Sarah had laughed at the thought of having a child at their age.

When I was sixteen years old, I had trouble with my brother Isaac, and Sarah tried to get my father to send my mother and me away. This he refused to do until God encouraged him to do so. We were sent away, with a little bread and a bottle of water, and we wandered in the wilderness until we were near death. My mother was ready to give me up to die when an angel of the Lord appeared, and directed us to some water and renewed God's promise of my future greatness. I prospered and took an Egyptian woman for my wife, but when my father Abraham died, I returned to help my brother bury him. I had twelve sons and lived to a ripe old age of 137.

All of the Arabs today trace their ancestry to my father, Abraham, through me, just as the Jews claim my father, Abraham, as their ancestor through my brother Isaac. If I might be granted one prayer it would be that through my brother Isaac, and me all of our descendants throughout the world might accept God's covenant of grace, which was given through the Lord Jesus Christ and live in peace.

SECTION I

THE WORD OF GOD FROM THE BEGINNING THROUGH PENTECOST

CHAPTER 1

THE WORD OF GOD

After, a lifetime of being a church member, and leading God's children, as a member of the church as Church member, and leading the church, as a teacher, Ruling Elder. Lay speaker, lay Preacher, and a certified lay Pastor, this is my understanding, of the power of the God's word.

God's word is the most powerful thing in the cosmic universe. By His word He can create, sustain, change or destroy. He created the universe. And He created mankind in His own image.

This is a synoptic of the use of, His word, from the time He created all things to the present, which the Holy

Spirit led me to write. It gives an orderly account of my understanding of the methods God used in dealing with civilization, which I call God's children.

It is my fervent prayer that each of you who read this, my writing, will be led, to give, your hearts to Jesus Christ, and he will fill your hearts with the Holy Spirit, as he has filled mine.

CHAPTER 2

THE WORD FROM
THE BEGINNING

In Genesis God spoke and created the world and created mankind in His, own image. We read where God spoke to Abram and changed his name to Abraham and made a covenant with him. Then we go to the book of Exodus where God spoke to Moses from the burning bush. When Moses, asked God, "who are you?" He said, "I am." God then told Moses to go back to Egypt and lead his people out of bondage. He said, "Tell them I am the Lord. I appeared to Abraham, to Isaac and to Jacob as God Almighty, but by my name I did not make myself known to them. Say therefore to the people of Israel, 'I am the Lord, and I will bring you out from the burdens of the Egyptians, and I will redeem you.'"

God sent plagues on the Egyptians, but they would not let the people go. So the Lord said to Moses, "Yet one more plague I will bring upon Pharaoh, and upon Egypt; afterward he will release your people. When he lets you go, he will drive you away completely."

And Moses said, "Thus says the Lord, about midnight I will go forth in the midst of Egypt, and all the firstborn in the land shall die." Thus he established the Passover.

The Lord told them through Moses to kill the Passover lamb and sprinkle the blood on their lintels and door posts. When the angel of death should appear he would pass over their houses, and the firstborn of their families would be saved. You shall observe this rite as an ordance for you, and your sons, for-ever. After this Passover, the Egyptians let the Israelites go, but when they arrived at the sea, the Egyptian army had followed them.

When the armies were about to attack the people the Lord said to Moses, "Lift up your hands over the sea, and divide it, that your people may go over on dry ground, through the sea." As they crossed the sea the Egyptian army came after them, but the Lord said to Moses, "Stretch out your hand over the sea, so that the waters come back upon the Egyptians." So Moses stretched out his hand, and the sea engulfed the Egyptian army.

When the people were in the wilderness they murmured against Moses, for they were without food, and the Lord said to Moses, "Behold, I will rain bread from heaven." In the evening quails came up and covered the camp, and, on the morning dew lay around the camp. When the dew had gone there was on the ground a fine, flake-like substance, fine as hoarfrost upon the ground, and the people asked, "What is it?" And Moses said to them, "It is bread from heaven, which the Lord has given you to eat." Thus the Lord saved them from starvation.

Later the Lord called Moses out of the mountain, saying, "Thus you shall say to the house of Jacob, 'You have seen what I did to the Egyptians and how I bare you on eagles' wings and brought you unto myself. Now, therefore, if you will obey my voice and, keep my covenant, you shall be My own possession among all people; for the earth is Mine, and you shall be a kingdom priests and a holy nation.' These are the words which you shall speak to the children of Israel."

Also in Exodus we read there was a violent storm, and the Lord called Moses to the top of the mountain. He gave the Israelites, through Moses, what we still call the ten commandments, saying, "I am the Lord thy God who brought you out of the land of Egypt, you shall have no other God's before me God's before me, you shall not make for yourself a graven image, you not take the name of the Lord your God in vain, remember the Sabeth day and keep it holy, honor thy Father and your Mother, you shall not kill, you shall not commit adultery, you shall not steal,; you shall not bear false witness; you shall not covet.

The people were afraid, and trembled and stood afar off. And Moses said to them, "Do not fear, for God has come to prove to you that you should fear Him, and not sin."

In the year King Uzziah died the world was rife with sin, and Isaiah also heard the voice of God. He wrote, "I heard the voice of the Lord saying, 'Who, shall I send, and who will go for me?' "Then I said, "Here, am I; send me."And he said, "Go and prophesy to the people," and Isaiah went and prophesied many times, warning the people to change their ways and return to their Lord and creator.

He also forecast the coming of a Savior, who would save the people from their sins. "The people who walked in darkness have seen a great light," and he said, "for to us a child is born, to us a son is given and His name will be called Wonderful, Counselor, Mighty God, Everlasting Father, Prince of Peace."

In the Old Testament we have many accounts of people hearing the voice, of the Lord, and in the New Testament Matthew starts out his Gospel announcing the birth of Jesus, of whom Isaiah had foretold. He wrote, "Now the birth of Jesus Christ took place in this way." Then he told us Mary had been engaged to Joseph, but before they came together she was found to be carrying a baby.

Joseph decided to divorce her without causing a stir, but an angel of the Lord appeared to him in a dream, saying, "Joseph, son of David, do not fear to take Mary as your wife, for that which is conceived in her is of the Holy Spirit. She will bear a son, and you shall call His name Jesus, for He will save His people from their sins." All this took place to fulfill what the Lord had spoken by Isaiah when he said, "Behold, a virgin shall conceive and bear a son, and His name shall be called Jesus, for He will save the prople from their sins."

Then Matthew went on to tell about the actual birth of Jesus, God incarnate.

Doctor Luke in his Gospel recounts the event that happened to the shepherds when Jesus was born and angels appeared to them in the field. They were afraid, but the angels said to them, "Be not afraid, for, behold, I bring you good news of great joy, which will come to all people, for to you is born this day in the city of David a Savior, who is Christ the Lord." And they heard the Heavenly Host singing, "Glory to God in the highest and on earth, peace among men with whom He is well pleased. "God spoke to them through an angel, and the heavenly host confirmed that this was a word from God.

We looked at the birth of Jesus, which fulfilled Isaiah's prophecy and was announced by an angel who appeared to the shepherds as they watched their flocks. We saw where Jesus began His earthly ministry, when John the Baptist baptized Him and heard the voice of God saying, "This is my beloved Son in whom I am well pleased."

When Jesus began His ministry He called certain people to be his Disciples. He called some by bidding them to follow Him, and, "he would make them to become fishers of men." In this section we remember the voice of God as spoken by His Son, Jesus Christ. The Gospels are replete with direct quotations of our Lord as He instructs us in the way we must live if we are to follow Him.

One thing Jesus tells us over and over is that God the Father loves us and we must also love His children. In Matthew 22 a lawyer asks Jesus, "Teacher, which is the greatest commandment?" and, he said to him, "you shall love the Lord your God with all your heart, and all your soul, and with all your mind. This is the great and first commandment, and a second is like it: You shall love your neighbor as yourself."

In Luke 10:25-28, a lawyer stood up to put Jesus to the test, saying, "Teacher, what shall I do to inherit eternal life." He said to him, "what is written in the law? How do you read?" and he answered, "you shall love the Lord with all your heart, and with all your soul, and with all your strength, and with all your mind, and your neighbor as yourself." He said to him, "you have answered right; do this, and you will live." But he desiring to justify himself, said to Jesus, "and who is my neighbor" then, Jesus told him a story about a merchant who was traveling along the thief-infested road to Jericho, when he was waylaid, stripped, beaten, robbed and left for dead. By chance, a certain priest came down the road and passed by the wounded merchant but offered him no assistance. Then, along came a Levite. He also passed the wounded man without stopping to see if he could help, even though he was of the same race as the man and the priest.

Then a Samaritan came along. The Samaritans were half-castes, a mixture of Jews and Gentiles, and were hated by the full-blooded Jews. The Jews would have no dealings with them and treated them as outcasts, but the Samaritan stopped, leaned over him and treated his wounds. He had compassion on him, poured oil and wine on his wounds and bound them, set him on his donkey, brought him to an inn and took care of him through the night. On the next day he gave the innkeeper money and told him, "Take care of him and anything he needs, and when I come again I will repay you." This is the way Jesus answered the lawyer's question of who was his neighbor.

In John chapter 13 Jesus gives us a new commandment, "a new commandment I give you, love one another as I have loved you."

Rev. Stedman Bryan, a special friend of mine and a former pastor, used to tell us often, "Love God, and love God's children." Jesus stressed this commandment by telling this story of the, good Samaritan.

Jesus also used parables when He told His followers the story of the lost sheep, which we find in Matthew 18. He said, "if a man has a hundred sheep, and one of them goes astray, does he not leave the ninety nine on the hill, and go in search of the one that went astray? And he finds it. Truly, I say to you, he rejoices over it more than over the ninety nine that never went astray. So it is not the will of my Father, who is in Heaven that one of these little ones should perish."

Jesus knew His mission here on earth was to take the sins of us all on Himself and to give His life as a ransom for our sins. He told His Disciples He was going away, but He would not leave them comfortless. He would send the Holy Spirit to live in their hearts, and the Holy Spirit would teach them all things, and bring, to their remembrance all, that he had told them.

He was tried on made-up charges and sentenced to die on the cross but God raised him on the third day. Jesus told us that," as the Father loved us so we must love one another." He gave us one last commandment, before He ascended into heaven to be with God the Father, where He intercedes for us. He gave us this commandment that we should, "go into the world and spread the good news of His gospel."

After He had ascended into heaven His Disciples felt lost without Him and His guidance. On the day of Pentecost they were huddled together in a room, not knowing where to turn or whom to turn to. Jesus kept His promise and sent the Holy Spirit, who descended on them like tongues of fire.

In the Acts of the Apostles Luke tells of this world-changing event. "When the day of Pentecost had come they were all together in one place. And suddenly a sound came from heaven like the rush of a mighty wind, and it filled the house where they were abiding. There appeared to them tongues as of fire, distributed and resting on each of them. Suddenly they were all filled with the Holy Spirit and began to speak, as the Spirit gave them utterance, and immediately they rushed out into the streets and began telling others this wonderful story of God's salvation.

Then Peter preached the first sermon of the Christian church: "Men of Israel, hear these words: Jesus of Nazareth, a man attested to you by God and with mighty works and wonders and signs, which God did through Him in your midst, as you yourself know, this Jesus, delivered up according to the definite plan and foreknowledge of God, was crucified and killed by the hands of lawless men. But God raised Him up, having loosened the pangs of death, because it was not possible for Him to be held by it." Now when the people heard this they were cut to the heart and said to Peter and to the rest of the apostles, "Brethren, what shall we do?"

And Peter said to them, "Repent, and be baptized, every one of you in the name of Jesus Christ for the forgiveness of your sins, and you shall receive the gift of the Holy Spirit." And fear came upon every soul, and many wonders and signs were done through the apostles, and, there were about 3000 souls who joined the church that day.

Jesus commanded us to go and speak in His name, and since that time the good news of salvation has been preached all around the world.

In our time He still speaks to us through the written word, through the ministry and through dedicated Christians. Have you heard God speaking to you as you read this wonderful account of salvation? Do you hear

God speaking to you? Are you listening? If so, what are you going to do about it? Won't you speak for God as you tell others this wonderful story of, how God has in the past and even today spoken to His children? As the old song goes, "Go and tell it on the mountain; go and tell it through the plains, wherever you find yourself, here, there and everywhere." Go and tell God's children.

CHAPTER 4

GOD'S WORD ACCORDING TO THE HOLY SPIRIT

Acts 1:43

This is the third in a series in which we are discussing the word of God. We looked first at the times God the Father spoke directly to some of His people; at other times when He spoke to them through a prophet, or spokesman, as He did when He promised us a Savior, or Messiah; and then other times when He spoke to us through an angel. In our last series we looked at some direct quotations of His Son, Jesus, as He spoke to us through Him, and we noted that Jesus taught us many things about the way we should conduct our lives. Sometimes using parables He told us stories about physical persons, things or circumstances to teach us spiritual lessons.

Jesus knew His chief purpose for coming to us was to save us from our sins, and He paid the supreme sacrifice for our sins when He was crucified on the cross. During His ministry He revealed that He was the Son of our God and Creator, and He taught us many things before He ascended back into heaven to be with the Father, there to intercede for us. He told His disciples that He was going away but would not leave them comfortless; He would send the Holy Spirit who would teach them all things and bring to their remembrance all, He had said to them.

In John 20:19-22, when He met His disciples after His resurrection, Jesus came and stood among them and said to them, "Peace be with you. As the Father sent me, so I send you. Go ye into the world and preach the gospel to all mankind." When He had said this He breathed on them and said to them, "Receive the Holy Spirit." In John 15:26-27 He again told them what to expect when the Holy Spirit came to them: "When the Comforter comes whom I will send to you from the Father, even the Spirit of truth, He will bear witness to me, and you are My witnesses because you have been with Me from the beginning."

In our last unit we discussed how the apostles reacted when the Holy Spirit descended on them at Pentecost, how they rushed out into the streets and began to witness, and how Peter on that day preached the first sermon of the Christian Church, on that day I call the birthday of the Christian church.

The church has grown from these few that witnessed the sending of the Holy Spirit at Pentecost to a worldwide congregation that has influenced the world and all who accept Jesus as their Lord and Savior.

In these last two thousand years millions of people have been led by the Holy Spirit to do God's work in the world. But I would like to draw your attention to three great Christians who were greatly affected by the leading of the Holy Spirit. First there was Saul, who was persecuting the church until the Spirit called him that day on the road to Damascus. God changed his name to Paul and called him to be the apostle to the Gentiles. He went on to become perhaps the greatest preacher and evangelist of all times.

And there was Simon who was the first to profess Jesus to be the Son of God. When Jesus asked, "Who do you say that I am?" Simon exclaimed, "You are the Christ, the Son of the living God." Jesus renamed him, Cepheus, being translated Peter. Jesus told him that "on your confession I will build my church." Peter denied Jesus three times on the night he was betrayed, but Jesus pardoned him. On

Pentecost, when the Holy Spirit descended on the apostles, Peter went out and preached the first Christian sermon, and the Christian church was born.

And we must point out Rev. Billy Graham, who founded one of the largest evangelistic organizations the world has ever known. He has preached at the four corners of the earth to millions of people.

The Holy Spirit called these three to carry out Christ's commission to go into the world and spread the good news of salvation to all people, and he is still calling men and women to go and share this wonderful story with others.

I would like to share with you an account of a case when the Holy Spirit changed the life of a man who became a dedicated Christian at a church where I was the pastor. Some years ago there was a married couple who belonged to my parish. The wife was very dedicated to the work of the church, but her husband seldom attended. One Sunday I preached a sermon on conversion. The husband, per chance, was in attendance. I used a true story about a man whose father was a successful banker. His son, who told me the story, had followed his father in the banking business. But when he met with success he began partying and drinking heavily, until he became a sot drunk and lost everything, including his will to work. He told me that when he was at his lowest the Holy Spirit came into his heart, and he stopped drinking and became a dedicated Christian, devoted to God and to God's children.

After he was filled with the Holy Spirit, he became a new person in Christ, and he became very active in the church. During the next year he was elected, and ordained an Elder, and served faithfully for his term, as a member. of the Session, for a three year term.

I, a humble, country preacher, accept no credit for the change in this person's life. To put it simply, his conversion was the work of the Holy Spirit.

This wonderful experience can be yours as well when you become submissive to the Word that became "flesh and dwelt among us, full of grace and truth" (John 1:14).

I sometimes think this part of the Bible is not emphasized enough. When we as Christians make our profession of faith and when pastors, ministers or lay preachers answer their ordination questions, we all profess to believe in God in three persons, including the Holy Spirit. But how often do you hear a preacher go into any detail explaining the work of the Holy Spirit?

Let me make this statement as clear as I can: If, it were not for being led by the Holy Spirit I could not prepare and preach to God's children every week. I am neither the smartest, nor the best educated person on the street, and I will admit there have been times when I did not know what to preach about. I have to keep reminding myself to rely on the Holy Spirit to teach me and guide me where He will have me go and what He would want me to say. Sometimes I simply scan through the Bible, and a passage jumps out at me. Other times I watch the news, and the Spirit guides me to bring certain items to the attention of the people. Or I may be reading, and something reminds me of a topic that a stressful society needs to hear. We live in a tense time. Sometimes when I retire for the night and say my prayers, I relax, and a message from God to His people suddenly comes from the Holy Spirit, and I sleep on it. The next morning I am ready to start reading, studying and lining up the service for Sunday morning.

In this series we have been looking at how God brings us His word. We know that in the old days He spoke to the people directly or through someone He called to speak for Him. Since the birth of His Son, Jesus, He has spoken through the second person of the Godhead, Jesus Christ. He doesn't speak in a vocal way through the Holy Spirit; He has sent Him to live in our hearts, to counsel and guide us. But if we will be attentive, and pledge to do His will, He will speak to us through other people, through that wee small voice within our hearts and, from the lips of those He has called to speak for Him.

There is one word of warning. In Matthew 12:31-32 we find this warning from Jesus: "Therefore, I tell you, every sin and blasphemy will be forgiven, but blasphemy against the Spirit will not be forgiven, and whoever says a word against the son of man will be forgiven, but whoever speaks against the Holy Spirit will not be forgiven, either in this age or the age to come."

We have been thinking about the powerful word of God. We receive His word by reading the Holy Scriptures, by hearing the Scriptures proclaimed and expounded upon, by hearing the witness of professing Christians and from the Holy Spirit.

Let us open our ears, our minds and our hearts to His word and go out and bear witness to the power of His word.

CHAPTER 5

THE HOLY SPIRIT COMES TO US

John 14:15-27

We presented our series on the word of God in four parts: first, the word as spoken to individuals by God Himself and through people whom He called to speak for Him; second, the word of God as spoken by Jesus, the second person of the Trinity; and third, as the promised Holy Spirit came to Jesus' followers. We looked at how they began to go out and speak to the people for God, how the Christian church was born when Peter preached the first Christian sermon on Pentecost and how the church grew from that handful of followers to become a worldwide religion.

There is in fact a fifth segment in this story of God's word. It starts immediately after the four Gospels in the book we call the Acts of the Apostles. This portion is not only about the book of Acts but runs throughout the rest of the New Testament. This we will call the acts of the called-out ones, who are led by the Holy Spirit.

Last week as I was reading I came across an article that reminded me of two quotations we have used in our series on the word of God. A former cowboy named Wagner stood in an area near the arena of a rodeo holding up a Bible in his left hand as he preached to a group of cowboys. Wagner, a Baptist preacher, was a former rodeo rider. He told them about his wild career. He was raised on a ranch and had fought, been beaten up, shot and stabbed. He had wrestled and boxed, but he started drinking.

"I was a saphead drunk," he said, "but my life was empty. I was looking for some meaning to my life. One day in the city jail I found myself reading the pages of the Bible. I saw that the Lord had established for me a home in heaven, and Jesus came into my heart." He read to them from 2 Corinthians 5:17: "Therefore if any man is in Christ, he is a new creature; old things have passed away; behold, all things are new." This is the miracle of the Holy Spirit. This former no-good drunk had been raised in a Christian home and attended church as a boy. He had some knowledge of the Bible but had put it all aside and gone the way of a careless drunk. But when he accepted Christ he received the Holy Spirit, and the Holy Spirit brought to his remembrance what he had heard and read in his youth, and he became a Baptist preacher, ministering to his former comrades. This story has been repeated multiple times as people are led by the Holy Spirit to change their lives.

This is what can and will happen in your life if and when you really and truly accept Jesus and His teachings. You will receive the Holy Spirit, He will bring all things to your remembrance, and all things will become new to you. This is what has been happening since that day at Pentecost when the Holy Spirit, who had been promised, descended on the apostles as they were huddled together, afraid and not knowing where to go, what to do or whom to go to.

This is the message I have for all mankind. Over the eons God speaks and is still speaking His word through His people. His word changes lives and makes all things new. This message is not nor ever will be completed. It will continue throughout the ages until that day when our Lord Jesus Christ returns and calls home all who trust Him to come, and reside with Him and His heavenly Father through all eternity. God bless you all while we await His coming.

CHAPTER 6

WE AS GOD'S CHILDREN
SPEAK TO HIM

Psalm 51 and Psalm 23

We have gone into considerable detail about how God speaks to us through the prophets, through Jesus, through the written word, through the preaching and expounding of the word, through the Holy Spirit and through our fellowman. But mankind also speaks to God when we go to Him in private or corporate prayer. One part of the Scriptures we have not touched on is the Psalms. Here the psalmist either speaks to God or speaks of Him with much admiration and respect. The Greek word for psalm is translated into English as song, so the book of Psalms is a book of songs acknowledging Jehovah, or God, to be the author, creator and sustainer of all things.

King David is credited with writing 74 of the 150 psalms. In Psalm 51, he asks God to have mercy on him and to blot out his transgressions. This was written after the prophet Nathan came to him and accused him of killing the husband of Bathsheba so he might have her for his wife. In this psalm David confesses his sin and asks God to restore to him the joy of salvation. He declares he will teach sinners the way of God, and they will be converted. And he prays to the Lord, "Open my lips, and my mouth will show forth thy praises." This is the contrite prayer of those who have sinned and been separated from their God; they are truly sorry for their sins and want God to forgive them and reconcile them with Him.

In Psalm 23 this same David, the former shepherd boy, thinks of himself as one of the master shepherd's sheep, for he fully understands how dependent the sheep are on the shepherd. He compares his own welfare with that of the sheep of a good shepherd. He starts out by acknowledging the Lord as his shepherd and says, "I shall not want." He shall not want for anything because the Lord will provide all his needs. He affirms that the Lord will see to his physical needs and his spiritual needs, restoring his soul. Then he says, "My cup overflows." By this he means he is so well protected and all of his needs, both physical and spiritual, provided for that he has an abundance of blessings.

Does your cup overflow? My cup overflows. I have been richly blessed all my life. Stop for a moment and count your blessings. Recognize how much God loves you and how He sent His Son, our Lord and Savior, to save you from eternal punishment and spiritual death for your sins. If you stop and count your blessings, you will realize how fortunate you are to live in the freest nation in the world. You have the freedom to worship without retribution or persecution and freedom to express your opinion without being punished or imprisoned.

I am sorry to say, that there are many in this land of ours, who would like to limit the freedoms, which our fore fathers put in the constitution, and the bill of rights, but we in the church must stand firm, and insist, that they do not alter our freedoms in any way.

Now tell me: Who says their cup is only half full or half empty? Can't we all say with David, "My cup overflows, surely, goodness and mercy will follow me all the days of my life, and I shall dwell in the house of the Lord forever."

May the Lord richly bless all His children, now, and, for evernore.

SECTION II

THE DISCIPLES OF CHRIST

CHAPTER ONE

DISCIPLESHIP

The word Disciple means; any follower of Christ, an adherent of the doctrines of another.

In this section we are going to look at some of the most noted Disciples of The Bible, and of the Christian era especially, those who were instrumental In the reformation, and the development of the reformed Faith, and the Churches, that comprises the Reformed Faith.

The writer of the Gospel of Matthew quotes Jesus when he gave us this Commandment, "All, authority in Heaven and on earth has been given to me, go, therefore and make Disciples of all nations, baptizing them in the name of the Father, and the Son and the Holy spirit, teaching them to observe all that I have commanded you, and, lo, I am with you to the close of the age."

CHAPTER TWO

FORWARD

I awoke early one morning, between Palm Sunday and Easter feeling sad, dejected, and rejected, because I had received so little response from my first book, *Mac's Mini-Bible*, I remembered in Luke 17:25, where Jesus said, "he must suffer, many things, and be rejected by his own generation."

In the book I had told all who would read my synopsis of the Bible, the story of how, God has dealt, and is dealing with his people, from the creation, up to the present. I wrote of how God had created the world, and created Mankind, in his own image, and how mankind had rebelled, and followed his own will, rather than following the will of God, but how God loved us still. And how he sent his own son to come, and teach us his will, and his way, because he still loved us, and how Jesus had come, and sacrificed himself, and died on the cross as the atonement for our sins.

Jesus chose twelve men to be his disciples, and they followed him for three years, before he was crucified, and God raised him from the grave. And his Disciples recognized him, and talked to him. One of the things he told them, was that he was going away, but he was not going to leave them in a mess, and, hopeless. That he would send them the Holy Spirit to comfort, guide, and council them. He promised us that if we would repent of our sins believe on him, and trust in him, that we would never die but would have eternal life. He told them that the Holy Spirit would, "bring to their remembrance all, that, he had told them." I came to my desk before dawn that morning feeling much relieved, and at peace, and began to write. So what, if people had not responded as I had hoped, and prayed they would.

During that same week of the year had not the people rejected my Master, and turned him over to the Romans, and when Pilot told the people that he would release one prisoner, as was his custom, they cried out, for him to release Barabbas, the thief, and when Pilot ask, what should he do with Jesus, they cried out, "crucify him, crucify him," and so they took him to the place called the skull, and hung him on a cross until he was dead, and he was buried in a borrowed tomb, but on the third day God resurrected him.

He met with his Disciples over a period of time, and was seen by many people who recognized him, as recorded in the New Testament. This is why I continue to write, that more people may hear this story, and believe, and be saved. In a few days I will conduct communion at two churches. I will share with you the communion meditation that I shared with the Churches.

CHAPTER THREE

HOLY COMMUNION

21 Luke 17:7-11, John 13:12-17 & 14:15

We meet around this table to celebrate Holy Communion, as Jesus instructed us, when he and his disciples gathered around the table on the night he was betrayed.

We come as his guests, even though he is not present in the flesh as he was when he ate his last supper with his Disciples, but he is certainly here with us in the spirit, because in John's Gospel, chapter fourteen he promised us that, even though he was going away, going back to the Father, who sent him, in order that he might become the sacrificial lamb, and die on a cross to pay the penalty for our sins. He said, "I will not leave you desolate, I will come to you. Yet a little while, and world will see me no more, but you will see me, because I live, you will live also'"

Then, in verses 25 through 27, he said, "these things, I have said to you, while I am still with you, but the councilor, the Holy Spirit, whom the Father will send in my name, he will teach you all things, and bring to your remembrance all that I have said to you. Let not your hearts be troubled, neither let them be afraid. Peace, my peace I give to you. Let not your heart be troubled, neither let then be afraid. You heard me say I am going, away, and I will come to you. If you love me, you will rejoice, because I go to the Father, for the Father is greater than I. I have told you this, before this occurs, so that the world may know, that I love the Father, and the Father loves you."

Also on the night he was betrayed some of his Disciples had been arguing about who was the greatest among themselves, and he gave them a final lesson on humility, when he stripped off his garments, put a towel around himself, and got a basin of water, and began to wash their feet.

John records this in his Gospel 13:4-7, "Jesus rose, and laid aside his garments, girded himself with a towel, and began to wash their feet." When he had washed their feet, and dried then with the towel, he put on his garments, and resumed his place, he said to them, "do you know what I have done to you? You call me teacher and Lord, and you are right, for so I am." If then your Lord and, teacher has washed your feet," you ought to be willing to wash each other's feet, and to serve each other, as I have served you. Truly, truly, I say to you, a servant is not greater than his master, nor is he who is sent greater than he who sent him. If you know these things, blessed are you, if you do them."

As we come to this, our Lord's Table, let us come as his humble servants. As we have stated, our Lord is not physically present, but let us come in humility, as the Holy Spirit guides us, not only on this grand occasion, but throughout our lives, as he has promised us salvation in his name. AMEN

And after our sermon just recorded I preached the following sermon.

MARK 16:4-20

I'm not going to ask for a show of hands, but how many of you know, or think you have been moved, or guided by the Holy Spirit, when you have a decision to make, on how to act, or react in certain circumstances?

Let's look at verses 15-20, where Jesus told his disciples, before he ascended back to his father, who had sent him to live among us, "go, ye into the world, and preach the Gospel to every creature. He said "the ones that believeth, and are baptized shall be saved, but the ones that believe not shall be damned," and in verse twenty, we are told, "they went forth, and preached everywhere the Lord working with them, and confirming the work with signs, following them."

This is why I know the Holy Spirit inspired me to write my book.

I hope you all have read it. Too many, of our ministers, and lay persons, when they preach, or tell others about Jesus stick to the Gospels, and tell others about Jesus, but ignore some of the passages in Acts, and the letters of the Apostles, which, speak so strongly about the work of the Holy Spirit. Without the guidance of the Holy Spirit I could not have written the first book.

I don't know if you have discovered that the books of the Bible tell a continuing story of, how God created the world, including mankind, who was created in his own image. That is to say, that we men and women were created spiritual creatures, not just another of the animals. God gave mankind dominion over all his creation, but mankind sinned, thus spoiling this Holy Image, and separating themselves from their Holy creator.

Through the Prophets God promised us a Savior, and sent his Son into the world as the atoning sacrifice for our sins.

Jesus promised us that if we repent of our sins, and put our faith and trust in him, that we will be saved. Jesus paid the supreme sacrifice for our sins, and promised us that after his departure he would send the Holy Spirit to be our guide and councilor, and he would bring to our remembrance all, that he had told us, and would teach us all things."

When the Holy Spirit came to the Disciples, they had been afraid of the Romans, who had crucified their Lord, and also of the leaders of the Jews, who had betrayed him, but when the Holy Spirit came to them, they lost their fears, and immediately ran out into the streets, and began telling everyone about Jesus. Peter, who had, earlier denied his Master three times, that night in the courtyard, filled with the Holy Spirit preached the first sermon, and the Christian Church was born.

Hearing his sermon, the people ask Peter, and the others, "what must we do?"And Peter told them, believe in their Lord Jesus Christ, repent of their sins, and be baptized in his name, and they would be saved. In Acts 2:41 Luke wrote, "those who were baptized were about three thousand souls."

CHAPTER FOUR

AFTER THE GOSPELS

In your Bible, after, the Gospels, for the balance of the New Testament tells us how Peter, Paul, John, and the other disciples carried the good news of salvation out into the world, and some of them recorded their words in letters to the Churches, as the Church began to grow, and spread all over the world.

According to the 2012 March issue of the National Geographic the Apostles traveled, preached and established Churches in different parts of the known world, and many of them were put to death for their faith.

James the greater was the first of them to die when King Herod had him beheaded. Traditions hold that eleven of them were martyred. Peter, Andrew, and Phillip were crucified, because of their faith, and, James, the lesser was beaten to death while praying for his attackers, Bartholomew, was flayed, and then crucified. Both, Thomas and Matthew were speared. Mathias was stoned to death, and Simon was either crucified, or sawed in half. John, the last surviving one of the twelve likely died peaceably, possibly in Ephesus, around the year one hundred.

The Apostles were the movement of the Church's cutting edge, spreading the message across the vast network of the ancient world, and leaving small Christian communities in their wake. This was the big bang moment for Christianity, with the Apostles blasting out of Jerusalem, and scattering across the known world. Thomas went east, through what is now Syria, and Iran, and historians believe. Then, on to Southern India. Mark, the evangelist also spread the message of Christianity, bringing Christ's message to Egypt, and founded the Coptic faith. We still speak of Thomas as doubting Thomas.

In the Gospel of John 20:29 Christ chastised Thomas, then, he said, "Thomas because you have seen me, you have believed, blessed are those who have not seen, and yet believe." His skepticism not withstanding Thomas still stands as the direct link between His converts in

Kerala, and on the founding of Christian Churches on the shores of the Mediterranean, unlike later groups in Asia, who were converted by missionaries, Thomas Christians believe the Church was founded by one of Christ's closest followers, and is central to Mark's Apostolic identity. They are an Apostolic Church.

Together these twelve who had followed Jesus three years during his earthly Ministry were at the forefront in carrying the good news of salvation out into the world, and Christianity became known throughout the world.

As we read the rest of the New Testament, see how true believers have obeyed Jesus commandment, by telling everyone who would listen, this most wonderful news, about what god did for us when he sent his son Jesus into the world

We aren't doing a very good job in the modern day Church, of proclaiming the good news of salvation, even though the church has a many layered program that they call evangelism. So many, who call themselves Christian either have not really received the Holy Spirit. Or, they are ashamed to admit that they are led by the Holy Spirit, Paul went into detail, in Romans, chapter one, where he wrote, I am not ashamed of the Gospel," and, in Romans 8: 26 he writes, "the Spirit helps us in our weakness for we do not know how to pray as we ought, but the Spirit intercedes for us with sighs too deep for words."

When we as Christians pray the prayer that our Lord taught us, we pray, Lord may thy will be done on earth, as it is in Heaven, too many times the sin of self will carries us along, instead of really seeking the will of God for our lives.

Satan, the arch enemy of God tempted Adam and Eve to eat of the tree of knowledge, the forbidden fruit, thus ruining their spiritual lives in Eden, and he will ruin your spiritual life, if you yield to his temptations.

In Matthew chapter sixteen, Peter began to rebuke Jesus, after Jesus had told his disciples how he would be crucified, and raised on the third day. Peter began to rebuke his Master, saying, "God, forbid, Lord, this will never happen to you, "But Jesus turned, and said to Peter, "get thee behind me, Satan, you are a hindrance to me. You are not on the side of God, but of men," then Jesus told his Disciples, if any man would come after me let him take up his cross, and follow me. For whoever would save his life will lose it, whoever loses their life, for my sake will find it, for what will it prophet a man, if they gain the whole world, and forfeit their life?"

This is why I write, as my way of trying to tell as many of God's Children this wonderful story of salvation as I can, and this is why I would like you to share my writings with as many others as you can. I realize, like my first book, I hope and pray that it gives a good account, as brief as it is, of this most wonderful news, that we find in the Bible, and how God has spoken to us through the Holy Trinity and through those who were inspired to record the word of God, and also those who share it with others.

May God bless each of you, where ever you are, and God bless his Holy Church now, and, for evermore.

CHAPTER FIVE

PAUL THE APOSTLE

When, we consider all who have endeavored to spread this good news of salvation. We must not leave out Paul, formally named Saul, who never followed Jesus during his earthy ministry. Instead when the Church began to grow, and attract more people after Pentecost, he was one of the Churches most zealous enemies, and stood by, and held the coats of those who stoned Steven to death. Saul went to the high priest, and asked for letters to the Jewish Synagogue at Damascus, so that if he found any belonging to the way, *any Christian's,* he might bring them bound to Jerusalem, for trail.

Now as he journeyed, he approached Damascus, and suddenly a light from Heaven flashed around him and he fell to the ground blinded, and he heard a voice, saying to him, "Saul, Saul, why do you persecute me? And he asked, "who are you Lord?' And was answered, "I am Jesus whom you are persecuting, rise and enter the city, and you will be told what you are to do."

When he arrived in the city he was approached by a man named Ananias, and Ananias laid his hands on Saul, and said, "brother Saul, the Lord Jesus who appeared to you on the road has sent me that you may regain your sight, and be filled with the Holy Spirit," and immediately, something like scales fell from his eyes, and he regained his sight. Then he arose, and was baptized, and took food, and was strengthened.

Saul was renamed Paul, and for the rest of his life he was an Apostle to the gentiles. Making journeys to much of the areas around the Mediterranean Sea, Preaching and organizing churches where ever he went. He also wrote letters to the churches, which were included in the New Testament. Paul was indeed a Disciple to Jesus, even if he never followed him during his earthly Ministry.

Most of the Disciples were uneducated men, much like I myself, but Paul had received much education, as is evident by his letters. Paul had a brilliant mind, a commanding knowledge of philosophy, and religion, and could debate with any of the educated scholars of his day. At the same time his understandable explanation of the gospel made his letters to the early Churches the foundation of, Christian Theology.

Paul had a zealous faith in our Lord and Savior, and described faith in his letter to the Hebrews, when he wrote in Heb. 11:1-3, "now faith is the assurance of things hoped for, the conviction of things not seen, for by it men of old received divine approval. By faith we understand that the world was created by the word of God, so that, what is seen, was made out of things which do not appear."

In his letter to the Roman's 5:1-3 he said, "Therefore, since we are justified by faith, we have peace with God, through our Lord Jesus Christ. Through him we have obtained access to this grace, in which we stand," and in his letter to Timothy,2d Tim 4:7 he seems one hundred percent satisfied with his faith when he writes, "I, have fought the good fight, I have kept the faith, I have finished the race."

Tradition portrays Paul as a physically small man. But he endured enormous physical handicaps on his missionary journeys.

We do not know what Paul called the thorn in his flesh, but he prayed three times, that the Lord remove this which he called a thorn in the flesh, but the only answer he got was when the Lord said to him, "my grace is sufficient for you, for my power is made perfect in weakness."

We affirm that even though Paul never followed Jesus during his earthly Ministry, that he was certainly a Disciple of Christ, as a disciple is anyone who is, an advocate of the doctrine of, another person, or God.

CHAPTER SIX

THE FIRST SPLIT IN THE CHURCH

The first split in the church came in 1054 A D. This was a slow process. In 330 AD Emperor Constantine decided to move the Capital, of the Roman Empire to the city of Byzeatinium, the capitol of modern Turkey, and called it Constantinople. In 1054, a formal split occurred, when Pope Leo IX excommunicated the Patriarch of Constantinople, thus, there was a major split in the Holy Catholic church.

Because of this split we call Constantine a Disciple, because what he did was to obey Christ in doing the work of the Church, by spreading, the good news of the Gospel.

The primary dispute that led to the split, between the Eastern Orthodox, and the Roman Catholic Church centered around, some deviation from the original conclusions of the seven Ecumenical Councils, such as the claim to a universal supremacy, a change had been made in the Nicene Creed in the sixth century. A change had been inserted into the Nicene Creed, thus changing the phrase pertaining to the origin of the Holy Spirit, from, who proceeds from the Father, to who proceeds from the Father, and the Son. Eastern Christians, believe both the Spirit, and the Son, have their origins in the Father.

CHAPTER SEVEN

MARTIN LUTHER, A DISCIPLE, AND REFORMER

Martin Luther was an avid Disciple who was born in Eisleben, Germany on 10 November1483, and died there on 18 February 1546. He was a Monk, Priest, and professor of theology writer, and, reformer. He became a public figure when he published in October 31, 1517, his ninety-five Theses; Latin propositions opposing the manner in which indulgencies, which were release from the penalties for sin, by the payment of money that were being sold in order for the building of Saint Peters in Rome.

Tradition has it that he nailed his Theses to the Church door in Wittenberg, his propositions were made public.

They caused great excitement, and were immediately translated into German, and widely distributed.

Luther's spirited defiance and further development of his position through public university debates in Wittenberg and other cities resulted in an investigation. The Roman Curia, summoned him, and condemned his teachings in June,15th, 1520,and summoned him demanded him to appear before Emperor Charles V, at the Diet of Worms in April. He was asked before the assembled secular and ecclesiastical rulers to recant. He refused firmly. The Pope demanded that he recant his Theses, and when he stood his ground, and refused to do so, he was excommunicated. After being banned by the Pope, Luther was taken to Wartburg Castle for refuge, and here he translated the New Testament, from Greek into German. He was one of the world's most rigorous Reformers of all time. We of the Protestant faith owe a great debt of gratitude to him, for what he did for the reformed faith, because of his leadership, and his writings.

CHAPTER EIGHT

JOHN CALVIN, A REFORMER, AND DISCIPLE

We Protestants owe, a great debt of gratitude to John Calvin, the French reformer who produced many sermons, and Biblical commentaries, letters, Theological treatises, and other works. Although nearly all of his adult life was spent in Geneva, his publications spread his ideas of a properly reformed Church to many parts of Europe, and from there to the rest of the world. He exerts a lasting influence over Christianity and western history.

At the age of twenty-six, Calvin published the first edition of his institutes of, the Christian Religion, A book that is still read by Theological students today. The book was written as an introductory text book on the Protestant Faith for those with some learning already, and covered a broad range of theological topics, from the Doctrines of Church, and Sacraments, to Justification by faith alone, and Christian Liberty, and it vigorously attracted the teaching of those Calvin considered strongly unorthodox, especially the Roman Catholic Church to which Calvin says he had been strongly devoted before his conversion to Protestantism.

Calvin developed his Theology, the most enduring component of his thought in Biblical commentaries, as well his sermons, and treatises.

Dutch Theologian Jacobus says; with regard to the values of Calvin's writings, next to the story of the Scriptures which I earnestly adulate, I exhort my pupils to peruse Calvin's commentaries, which I extol in lofty terms, that he excels beyond comparison in the Interpretation of Scripture and his commentaries ought to be more highly valued than all that is handed to us by the liberty of the Father, so that I acknowledge him to have passed above most others, or rather above all other man.

He wrote a short treatise on the Lord's Supper in 1540, but it was written in French, so it was less accessible to the scholastic readers of the time. Martin Luther found a copy of the book in Latin, in a book store, later in his life, and commented, that he could have entrusted the whole controversy of the last supper to Calvin from the beginning.

CHAPTER NINE

A DISCIPLE, FROM SCOTLAND; JOHN KNOX

Let us not overlook John Knox, who is considered to be the greatest reformer in the history of Scotland. The exact place of his birth is not known with certainty, but it is generally accepted to be Gifford, sixteen miles east of Edinburg, and he is the author of, The History of the Reformation in Scotland.

He attended the University at Glasgow, but how long he remained at collage is uncertain. He was ordained to the Priesthood at some date prior to 1540. He first professed the Protestant faith about the end of 1545, and was first called to the Protestant Ministry at St. Andrews, which was throughout his life intimately associated with his career as a reformer.

For a time he served as a minister, of an English Church, and in August 1555 he returned to Scotland where he remained for nine months preaching Evangelical Doctrine in various parts of the country and persuading those who favored the Reformation to cease attending Mass, and to join with himself in the celebration of the Lord's supper according to a reformed ritual.

When the reformed Protestant religion was formerly ratified by law in Scotland in 1560 he was appointed Minister of the Church of St. Giles, then the main Church at Edinburg. He was at this time in the fullness of his power, as is manifest abundantly in his," History of the Reformation," a work which appears to have begun about 1559, and completed in the course of six, or seven years, They are works of true genius, and well worthy in their character of the great leader, and statesman who wrote them.

In his later years he lived a very busy life, as he was much engrossed with the public affairs of the national Church, and at the same time devoted to his work as a parish Minister. He lived in kindly relations with his neighbors, many of whom, in every rank, were among his close friends.

On the monument at his grave are imprinted these words, "here, lyeth a man who in his life never feared the face of man, who hath been often threatened with danger, but yet hath ended his days in peace and honor.

CHAPTER TEN

THE DIVISIONS WITHIN THE PROTESTANT CHURCH

After a split between the Roman Catholic Church and the Protestants, Protestants began to split into different Churches or Denominations within the Church, but their differences were more about the form of government, than differences in theology, they all hold the same beliefs on the authority of the Bible, and they celebrate the same sacraments of baptism, and Holy Communion, though they might disagree about the mode of baptism.

Some of them totally immerse the precipitants, while others pour water on their heads, and others sprinkle water on their heads, but all baptize in the name of the Father, the Son, and the Holy Spirit, as Jesus commanded us to do.

Some, like the Baptists have a democratic form of government, where they are led by, the Minister, and the Board of Deacons. They have a one person, one vote decision on all major decisions on Church matters.

Others have a republican form of government, where each congregation elects Elders, both Ruling Elders, and Teaching Elders, or Ministers to represent them on most matters in the local Church, and to represent them in all higher courts, such as the Presbytery, the Synod, and the General Assembly

Others have a system of government similar to that of the Roman Catholic Church in which, orders, and directives are handed down by Bishops to the local Churches.

Aside from these minor differences, they all believe in salvation by the grace of God, through Our Lord and Savior Jesus Christ, who came and gave His life for the atonement of our sins.

CHAPTER ELEVEN

PRESBYTERIAN DISCIPLES

The roots of Presbyterianism can be traced to the Theology of John Calvin, the leader of the Protestant reformation in Geneva, here. Calvin sought to establish a Church government based on the New Testament concept of the office of Elder.

John Knox carried this form of Church government into Scotland, and is credited with establishing the Church of Scotland which became the Presbyterian Church, and the Scots brought Presbyterianism to the colonies, which are now The United States.

My ancestors brought their Religion here to what is now called, the Cape Fear valley. They brought their Bibles, but had no Preacher.

Frances Mackie, a Scottish, Presbyterian Minister came to the Colonies in 1683, and is generally considered the Father of American Presbyterianism.

The Rev. James Campbell came to the Cape Fear Valley in North Carolina in 1757 and in 1758 he accepted a call to be the regular Minister of the Scottish settlers, and entered into a contract with them.

In that same year the Churches of Barbecue, Long Street, and Bluff, were Organized, thus bringing Presbyterianism to this part of what is now North Carolina, where I have lived all of my 87 years.

Barbecue and Bluff are still active churches in Coastal Carolina Presbytery, but when the Government acquired the property for Fort Bragg, North Carolina, Long Street was in the reservation. The army maintains the Church building, and the cemetery Malcolm Fowlers book, *they passed this way*

Certainly, Francis, and James Campbell were devout Disciples of our Lord.

CHAPTER TWELVE

JOHN WESLEY, METHODIST DISCIPLE

John Wesley was an English Theologian. He was ordained Deacon in 1775, and was admitted to the Priesthood in the Church of England in 1728.

On May 24 1728, he experienced a religious awakening, that convinced him, that salvation was possible, for any person, through faith in Jesus Christ, and he alone can offer salvation.

He became an Evangelist, and attracted immense crowds, from the outset of his evangelistic career

In May 1739, he and a group of his followers formed the first Methodist society.

Wesley designated lay Preachers to serve Churches, and called the first conference of, Methodist leaders, to meet in 1744.

He was a tireless Preacher, delivering as many as five sermons a day, on certain occasions.

He compiled twenty three collections of hymns and his personal journal< 1735-1790> is outstanding, for his frank exposition on the spiritual development, of a child of God.

All Protestants, especially Methodists, owe a great debt of gratitude to John Wesley, a true Disciple of our Lord.

CHAPTER THIRTEEN

THOMAS HELWYS, AND JOHN SMYTH

Thomas Helwys, and John Smyth founded the first Baptist Church on Dutch soil at Amsterdam in, or around 1609, and in 1611, Helwys led a small group of Christians in establishing the first Baptist Church near London, England

From their base in England, Baptist's have grown to number nearly one million members, in England, but it was in America, however, that Baptist experienced their greatest growth, and now Baptist's in America number over twenty eight million.

Thomas Helwys, and John Smyth didn't immediately make a huge impact in the Church they founded, but they were strong Disciples of Our Lord.

CHAPTER FOURTEEN

BILLY GRAHAM, A MODERN DAY DISCIPLE

We owe a great debt of gratitude to Rev. Billy Graham, a modern day Disciple, whose sermons have been heard in person, on the radio and T V, and by the means of the recorded media, and read by more people than any Preacher in the modern world.

In April, 2013, Rev. Graham was honored by the State Legislature as, North Carolina's favorite son.

CHAPTER FIFTEEN

TRUE DISCIPLESHIP

All of these written about in this section were true Disciples of our Lord

Discipleship is what has grown the Church, from those Apostles, who became Disciples on the day of Pentecost when the Holy Spirit came, as Jesus had promised. The Church has grown, from the five thousand who accepted Jesus, and repented on that day of Pentecost to encompass the world.

This, is the work of the Holy Spirit, working in the hearts of more and more people, as they become Disciples, and go out, and obey the command of their

Lord when he told us to go, and, "make Disciples of all nations"

If and when you accept Jesus as your Lord, and Savior, you become a Disciple, but far too many accept Jesus, as their Lord, and do not become active Disciples, and do not go out, and make Disciples of others along the way.

"What the Church needs are active Disciples, who are obsessed by the Holy Spirit to go out and make Disciples of others along the way,

CHAPTER SIXTEEN

MAC, AN OLD DISCIPLE WRITES

All of those who follow Christ and pattern their lives after him and his teachings receive the Holy Spirit. All the simple, the Fishermen, and the educated, and the in between

Writers, Professors, Ministers, and dedicated followers of Christ were, and are disciples in the true sense.

You too may become a disciple, since a disciple is any follower of Christ, who adheres to his doctrine.

If you decide to follow him, and his teaching, you will become a Disciple of his, and, he will send the Holy Spirit to live in your heart and council, and guide you. I know

I'm just another one of his Disciples. I don't have a high degree of scholastic learning like Paul, Martin Luther, Calvin, or Knox, but I do, follow his teaching, and preach them to his children.

In the next chapter we will look at some of my teachings.

CHAPTER SEVENTEEN

TWO SERMONS BY AN OLD DISCIPLE, MAC

Genesis 17:1-8, Acts 2:37-39, Titus 1:1-4, James 12:12-5

We have read some of the promises that God made to mankind, and some of the covenants between God, and certain individuals, or people in general.

Let's look at the difference in a promise, and a covenant. You promise to keep your word, and fulfill what you have promised. A promise is a declaration made to another, with respect, to the future, giving the assurance, that you will do, or not do, give, or not give something to, or for some one.

A covenant is an agreement between two, or more persons, to do, or refrain from doing some act, much like a contract, between persons, or an agreement, or contract, between certain parties, or in this case an agreement between God, and mankind.

Anyone can sometimes get by when they make a promise, but when you make a covenant, or contract, and break it, there may be dire consequences.

Such as when you buy some land, or property, and you contract to pay at a certain time, or at certain intervals. There are perhaps nearly a million homes right now in foreclosure, because the covenant between the buyer and the seller, or finance company was broken. Have you ever made a promise to a friend, family member, or someone else, and broken your promise, and the other person was left holding the bag, or they were hurt or maybe their feelings toward you were damaged and your friendship deteriorated?

When I was a teenager, and was going to the store I promised my younger brother I would bring him some candy, and when I, came home, empty handed it broke his heart, because I hadn't kept my promise, and he cried all night.

This kind of thing happens all too often in the times we now live.

When I was a youngster many deals were made without any written record of the deal. Many trades and deals were settled with just a shake of hands. Don't try that now, unless you wish to end up settling your deal in front of a Judge, and Jury.

In our text we saw some of the promises God made to his children and where he made a covenant with Abram, and changed his name to Abraham He covenanted with him, that he would be his God, and that all mankind would be blessed through him, if they would worship him and, follow his way, but these descendants decided to follow their own wills, God still loved his people, and would not just give up on them, so God, through his Prophets promised to send them a Savior, and kept his promise when he sent his Son Jesus into the world to atone for our sins.

When Jesus was about thirty years old he began his earthly ministry, and taught us the way we should live, and went to the cross to make retribution for our sins.

Before he was crucified on the Roman cross, he made another promise, when he told his disciples, "that he was going away, but he would not leave them comfortless, and without hope. Because he would send the third person of the Trinity; the Holy Spirit, who would teach them all things, and bring to their remembrance all, that he had told them, through Jesus."

When the Holy Spirit kept his promise, and came to the Apostles at Pentecost, they, filled with the Spirit ran out into the streets, and began obeying the command, that Jesus had given them, when he said, "go, ye into the world, and make disciples of all nations."

I would remind you that even if we sometimes break a promise, neither our Heavenly Father, or His Holy Son ever break a promise, or go back on a covenant,

We break our promise, if, and when we join the Church, and then. Let our self will overpower the will of God, and do not share our religious experience with God's children. This is why the Holy Catholic Church; the Church universal, is in decline, when it should be growing by leaps and bounds, When we accept the promise of eternal life, we must not let our own selfish wills overpower the will of God in our lives.

If we make a profession of faith and promise to follow Jesus and his teaching, and let our selfishness rule our lives, instead of following Jesus, and doing his will, we become like the Pharisees, and hypocrites, don't we?

I don't think we need to be reminded, that during each service of worship when saying, the Lord's Prayer; we pray to the Lord, Thy will be done, on earth, as it is in Heaven. If we would take this serious, and attempt to do his will, instead of insisting, that we live according to our own selfish wills, and live the way the Holy Spirit guides us, then his will shall be done on earth as is in heaven

Matthew 5:1-16

Will we ever see God?

In the Gospels we have the record of untold numbers of, people who walked, and talked with Jesus. We read of him being followed by multitudes, and we have countless quotations of his, recorded by those who followed him during his Ministry here on earth, but, will we ever see God the Father?

Yes, let me assure you that someday, if we put our faith and trust in Jesus, who came into the world as God incarnate; fully God, yet also fully human as we are, then some day we will be in God's presence forever, and we will see him in all his greatness, and glory.

In our scripture lesson we read where Jesus said, "Blessed are the pure in heart, for they will see God. This is why I preach each Sunday, and, urge everyone to put their faith and trust in Jesus, because he was sent by the Father to live among us, and die for our salvation. If we put our full dependence on Jesus, then he will pardon all our sins, and that's the only way we will ever become pure in heart, and be able to go to Heaven, when god calls us to come. Even though I desperately urge you to do this, so you can go to Heaven, and meet your creator, and your God there, I can't imagine what that will be like; not, really, because, Heaven will be far greater than I can ever imagine. Far greater than anything we presently know.

In some ways Heaven may be like our lives right now. We may live in a place somewhat like this world, where we now live, although a place without sin, or decay, a place, where we will have no pain, or sorrow, a place where there will be no coveting, no more grief, no more shame, but a place of joy, and happiness.

In other ways it will be far more, beautiful, and glorious than anything we've ever experienced. One reason is, because we will be in the presence of God forever. Like the shepherds to whom the Angel came on that first Noel. When we first glimpse Heaven I'm sure we'll be over-whelmed by the power and glory of God.

We in our present state of sin have no right to be in God's presence in Heaven, because we are sinful, and impure in heart, and God is absolutely Holy and pure, but

Jesus Christ came into the world for one reason alone; to cleanse us from our sins, so we could go to Heaven when we die. He did this by becoming the, final, and complete sacrifice for our sins, through his death on the cross. Some day your life here on earth will be over. Are you prepared for that day? Are you really ready? Have your sins been forgiven, so you are pure in heart?

Don't delay for one hour, because Jesus said that no one knows the hour when the son of man will come, not even the Angels in Heaven, but only the Father knows. So, again, do not delay, but put your faith and trust in Jesus, and he alone, for your salvation, and then rejoice, that someday you will be in God's presence, and you will meet him face to face. What a glorious day that will be.

ABOUT THE AUTHOR

I, Ishmael "Mac" McDonald was born in Harnett co. NC on the 3rd of November 1925, the son of a farmer William Hawley McDonald. I grew up as a very introverted person, because I was ashamed of my name.

Rev. Frank Wilkerson helped me to overcome my shyness, and encouraged me to start preaching, as a layman. I was certified by Carolina Coastal Presbytery, and have been serving Churches in my area for thirty years, and was elected Pastor Emeritus of Palestine Presbyterian Church, where I still help out when needed.